INTERESTING FACTS ABOUT THE
EMPIRE STATE BUILDING
ENGINEERING BOOK FOR BOYS

Children's Engineering Books

BABY PROFESSOR
EDUCATION KIDS

Speedy Publishing LLC
40 E. Main St. #1156
Newark, DE 19711
www.speedypublishing.com

In this book, we're going to talk about the Empire State Building in New York City. So, let's get right to it!

Manhattan downtown skyline with illuminated Empire State Building and skyscrapers at sunset.

When the Empire State Building was built, it became the tallest building in the world. Other buildings have since surpassed it in height, but it remains a famous landmark in New York City with its towering and beautiful Art Deco style. It's been included as a plot element in many movies, such as the monster movie *King Kong* and the romantic comedy *Sleepless in Seattle.* Millions have been made from the merchandising of its image for toys, postcards, posters, and ashtrays.

King Kong movie scene, 1933.

THE RACE TO TOUCH THE SKY

The Eiffel Tower in Paris seemed like it would touch the sky with its 984-foot height. It was the tallest building in the world when it was built in 1889. Architects in the United States were inspired by the tower. It was time to take the *"Tallest building in the world"* honor away from the French.

View of Eiffel tower and bridge

Looking down on old New York skyscrapers.

By the beginning of the twentieth century, an unannounced race was on for which architects and building developers could create the tallest structure. First, in 1909, the Metropolitan Life building was built. At 700 feet tall and 50 stories high, it was

certainly a skyscraper, but still not as tall as the Eiffel Tower. It was followed by the 792-foot tall Woolworth Building, built in 1913, and the Bank of Manhattan building, built in 1929, at 71 stories and 927 feet high.

Then, two equally ambitious men got into the skyscraper race. Walter Chrysler, who was Chrysler Corporation's founder, and John Jakob Raskob, a former General Motor's vice president, were car-company rivals and each wanted the distinction of the tallest building in the great city of New York.

Walter P. Chrysler at the White House

Chrysler was already constructing a monumental building, but he had kept the height of the building a secret. Raskob began plans for the construction of his own building, but he didn't know what height his building had to reach before it would be taller than Chrysler's.

The Chrysler Building was the world's tallest building (319 m) before it was surpassed by the Empire State Building in 1931

John J. Raskob

Right before the Great Depression, in 1929, Raskob along with his business partners bought a piece of property where the Waldorf-Astoria Hotel was situated. Real estate had grown tremendously in value and the owners of the hotel had decided that they wanted to sell the land and build a new hotel at a site on Park Avenue. Raskob bought the property at 34th Street and Fifth Avenue for about $16 million.

THE BUILDING PLAN

Now it was time to hire an architectural firm and get his plan in place. Raskob decided upon the firm of Shreve, Lamb, & Harmon as his new architects. Legend had it that Raskob took a very thick pencil out of a drawer and then held it vertically as he spoke to William Lamb. Raskob said, *"How high can it be so it won't fall down?"*

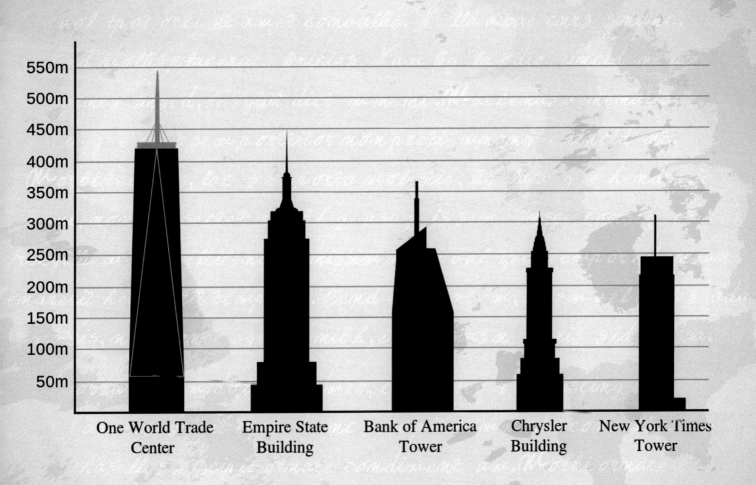

Height comparison of New York City buildings,
with Empire State second from left.

Lamb just smiled and started the work to create the skyscraper's design. Inspired by the pencil shape, the design Lamb created had the sleek, streamlined look of Art Deco with stepped up sides that were vaguely like a pyramid. The center of the building would house the elevator shafts, mail chutes, restrooms, and corridors.

Looking at the sky between skyscrapers in New York City.

The perimeter of the space for offices was to be 28 feet deep. As the number of elevators decreased, the floors would get smaller in size. The space that wasn't rentable was surrounded by the space that was rentable. Observatories where visitors could view the city from the top would be placed from the 86th to the 102nd floor.

View from Empire State Building

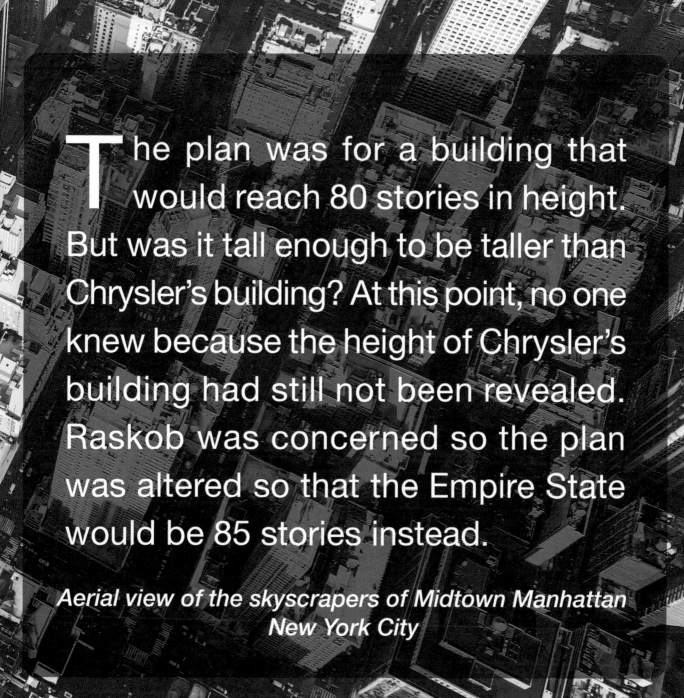

The plan was for a building that would reach 80 stories in height. But was it tall enough to be taller than Chrysler's building? At this point, no one knew because the height of Chrysler's building had still not been revealed. Raskob was concerned so the plan was altered so that the Empire State would be 85 stories instead.

Aerial view of the skyscrapers of Midtown Manhattan New York City

Raskob was still afraid that the design, which was about four feet higher than the proposed Chrysler building would be trumped at the last minute. He was concerned that the competitive Walter Chrysler would find a way to put a steel pole in his building's spire and make it taller than Raskob's building at the eleventh hour.

At 1,046 feet (318.9 m), spire, crown and facade of the Crysler Building

After looking at a model of the building, Raskob suggested that the building could use a top hat, which could be built as a dirigible docking station. Although this idea of a docking station never worked as planned, the *"hat"* brought the height of the building from 1,250 feet to 1,454 feet.

Aerial view over Manhattan with Empire State Building and World Trade Center

WHO WERE THE BUILDERS?

Raskob and the architects began to interview the potential construction companies for the completion of the building. Raskob needed the building to be done as quickly as possible so that he could rent offices and make income. The company of Starrett Brothers and Eken were one of the companies interviewed.

Sunset in New York, Empire State Building

When asked how much equipment the company owned that they would use, Paul Starrett answered that they didn't even have a single shovel!

He told Raskob that standard building equipment was not going to work for their unique building. Instead, he said that he and his team would buy the newest available technology, customize it for the job, and then sell it when the building was complete and credit Raskob for any difference.

New York City - United States of America

S tarrett suggested that this approach would cost less than other methods and he committed to an incredibly fast 18-month completion schedule. Impressed by their honesty, fast schedule, and quality, Raskob awarded them the job.

The Empire State Building entrance hall decorations, New York City

With this very tight schedule, it was essential that every minute be used well. The construction team immediately started to hire the appropriate subcontractors. They ordered the customized supplies to the exact specifications and hired companies they knew would follow instructions consistently and be able to produce the high-quality construction. The timetable was planned so that each process needed for the building overlapped in order to save the most time possible.

New York City at night, view toward south with Rockefeller center and Empire State Building, 1930s

New York City, view south of lower New York skyline from the Empire State Building. Ca. 1931

DEMOLISHING THE OLD TO MAKE WAY FOR THE NEW

The first order of business was to demolish the old hotel. When the public heard that the building was going to be torn down, many of them wrote asking for mementos of their trips or honeymoons. There were requests for keys, fireplaces, and stained glass windows. An auction was held and then the rest of the hotel was torn down.

Building rubble showing the demolished bricks and mortar of the construction.

A majority of the building debris was loaded onto ships and dumped out in the Atlantic Ocean.

The excavation for the new building's foundation was begun before the hotel was completely torn down. Six hundred men worked in two shifts of 300 at a time to dig through the bedrock for the massive foundation that was needed.

THE STEEL SKELETON

Work began on the skeleton of steel in March of 1930. The vertical frame of the structure was made of 210 steel columns, 12 of which ran almost the entire building height, except for the very top mooring mast. Other steel sections were 6 to 8 stories long.

Middle aged iron worker at the Empire State Building construction site, 1930. The Chrysler Building's spire is at right.

These enormous girders made of steel couldn't be raised up more than 30 stories in one pass, so numerous cranes, called derricks, had to be used to pass them up to the floors above the 30th story.

As the construction was going on, pedestrians walking in the street below would gaze up in awe as workers defied death by crawling, walking, and swinging on the giant steel frames.

Empire State Building Girders and Workers

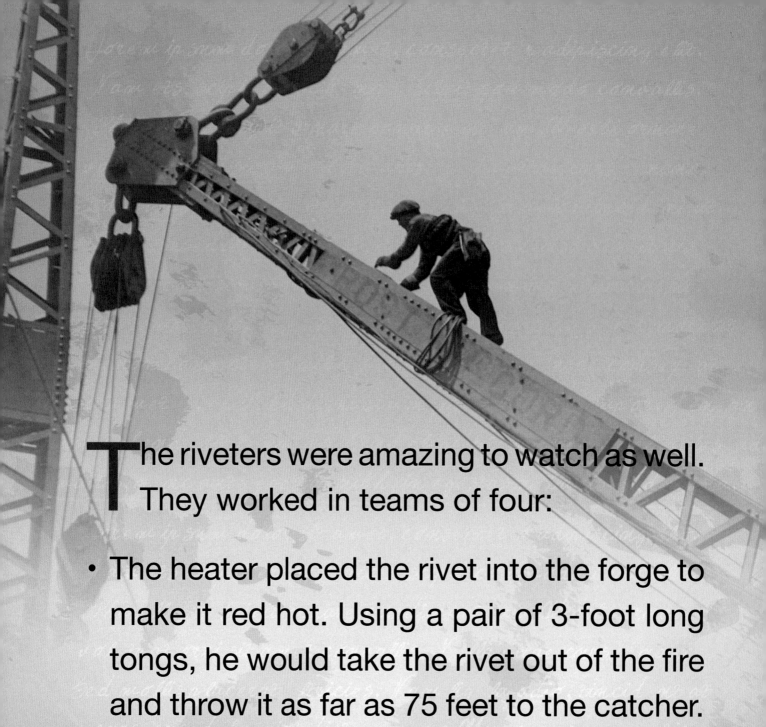

The riveters were amazing to watch as well. They worked in teams of four:

- The heater placed the rivet into the forge to make it red hot. Using a pair of 3-foot long tongs, he would take the rivet out of the fire and throw it as far as 75 feet to the catcher.

- The catcher would use a discarded paint can to catch the red-hot rivet. With his other hand, he would use tongs to take it out and pound it against the frame to remove any cinders. Then, he would place it into a hole.

Scaffolding with a worker on top working on the entry of the Empire State Building

- The bucker-up would support the rivet in place.

- The gunman would pound in the rivet with a special hammer that used compressed air.

These teams worked from the bottom floor all the way up to the 102nd floor. The very last rivet pounded in was made of solid gold.

EFFICIENT COORDINATION

The builders of the Empire State Building came up with unique ways to save time and manpower during the construction. They had railway cars to move materials back and forth. The construction required over 10 million bricks and Starrett devised a way to move the bricks using chutes and hoppers in the basement. This eliminated the need to close down the streets near the construction site.

Construction workers raising up steel.

JUN. 26 30   JUL. 7 30   JUL. 24 30   AUG. 18 30   SEPT. 8 30   NOV. 10 30

The construction phases of the Empire State Building.

Once they got their *"Assembly Line"* going, the men were able to erect over fourteen floors in just ten days including the steel frame and concrete.

The elevator construction was another marvel of engineering. There were seven banks of elevators. Each of them serviced only a portion of floors. In this way, depending on where you were in the building, you would only have to go through a section of floors to get to the top.

They installed faster elevators, but couldn't use their top speed until the building code changed from 700 feet per minute to 1,200 feet per minute. Once the code changed, they sped the elevators up!

Interior of the Empire State Building.

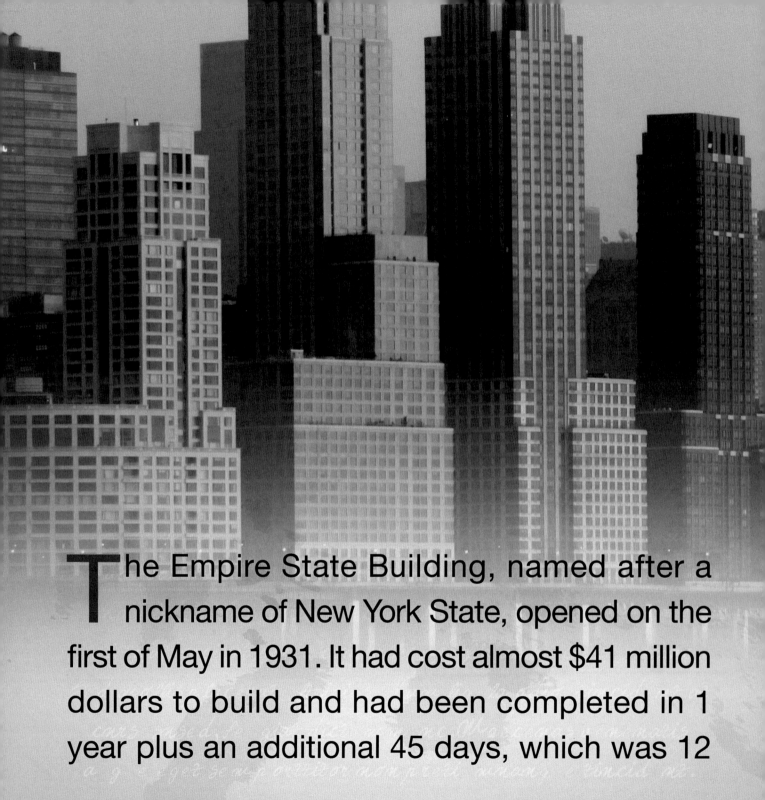

The Empire State Building, named after a nickname of New York State, opened on the first of May in 1931. It had cost almost $41 million dollars to build and had been completed in 1 year plus an additional 45 days, which was 12

1930s look of midtown Manhattan skyline.

days ahead of the proposed schedule. President Herbert Hoover pushed a button to light up the tower. It would be the tallest building in the world for 40 years and a source of inspiration during the Great Depression.

Awesome! Now you know more about how the Empire State Building, one of the most famous and beautiful buildings in New York City, was built. You can find more Engineering books from Baby Professor by searching the website of your favorite book retailer.

Illuminated signs of The Store in the Empire State Building

Visit

BABY PROFESSOR
EDUCATION KIDS

www.BabyProfessorBooks.com
to download Free Baby Professor eBooks
and view our catalog of new and exciting
Children's Books

Made in the USA
Middletown, DE
18 January 2020